for one or two

simple and delicious easy-to-make recipes

Bernice Hurst

p

This is a Parragon Publishing Book
First published in 2002

Parragon Publishing
Queen Street House
4 Queen Street
Bath, BA1 1HE, UK

ISBN: 0-75258-895-8

Printed in China

Produced by the Bridgewater Book Company Ltd.

Photographer Simon Punter

Home Economist Ricky Turner

Cover
Photographer Ian Parsons

Home Economist Sara Hesketh

NOTES FOR THE READER

- This book uses both imperial and metric measurements. Follow the same units of measurement throughout; do not mix imperial and metric.

- All spoon measurements are level: teaspoons are assumed to be 5 ml, and tablespoons are assumed to be 15 ml.

- Unless otherwise stated, milk is assumed to be whole milk, eggs and individual vegetables such as carrots are medium, and pepper is freshly ground black pepper.

- Recipes using raw eggs should be avoided by infants, the elderly, pregnant women, convalescents, and anyone suffering from an illness.

- The times given are an approximate guide only. Preparation times differ according to the techniques used by different people and the cooking times may also vary from those given. Optional ingredients, variations, or serving suggestions have not been included in the calculations.

contents

introduction

Cooking for one or two provides an opportunity for experimentation and creativity without too much wastage. It enables you to try out new ingredients and recipes on a small scale so that you can decide what you do and don't like (in terms of ingredients, combinations, and method) and calculate how to make amendments or improvements next time. You have only yourself, and perhaps one other, to please.

If you believe that food is something to be enjoyed, and frequently shared, then cooking for one or two is the time to perfect your ideas and cooking skills.

The recipes in this book can easily be increased or decreased so that any one of them is suitable for one, two, or more if you decide to invite a few friends to dinner.

As with most cookbooks, this one has a selection of recipes that should not only make delicious dining but, hopefully, provide inspiration and give you the confidence to create your own dishes.

guide to recipe key	
easy	Recipes are graded as follows: 1 pea = easy; 2 peas = very easy; 3 peas = extremely easy.
serves 2	Recipes serve one or two people, as stated in each recipe. When adapting to make more or less, take care not to mix imperial and metric measurements.
10 minutes	Preparation time. Where chilling or marinating is involved, the time needed is shown separately: eg, 10 minutes + 30 minutes to chill.
30 minutes	Cooking time.

pan-braised chicken,
page 10

cured ham with glazed sautéed
pineapple, page 42

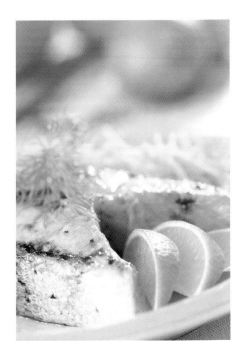

broiled lemon salmon,
page 60

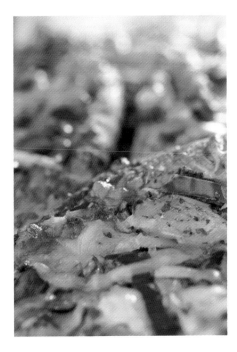

basic pizza dough & pizza topping,
page 94

poultry

When cooking poultry for one or two people, you can either select the cuts that you need or buy a whole bird, then cut it into portions, and prepare those portions separately in a number of different ways. Chicken, turkey, and duck all lend themselves well to recipes that are quick and easy or long and slow (but not necessarily difficult). The meat combines well with sweet ingredients, as in Broiled Chicken & Pineapple, and with hot spices, as in Spicy Bell Pepper Chicken or Broiled Mexican Chicken, while dishes, such as Crispy Crumb Turkey bring out the full flavor of the meat.

broiled chicken
& pineapple

		ingredients
	very easy	MARINADE 1 tbsp olive oil juice of 1 lime
	serves 1	
	5 minutes + 30 minutes to marinate	1 skinless, boneless chicken breast portion 2 pineapple slices 1 tbsp butter, melted
	20 minutes	cooked snow peas, to serve

Combine the oil and lime juice in a glass dish. Place the chicken in the dish, stir well to coat in the marinade, cover with plastic wrap, and chill in the refrigerator for 30 minutes, turning once.

Remove the chicken from the refrigerator. Discard the marinade.

With the broiler at high, cook the chicken on the rack, skin side up, for 5 minutes, or until brown. Reduce the heat to medium and cook for 5 minutes more. Turn and cook for 10 minutes on the second side.

When you turn the chicken to cook on the second side, brush the pineapple slices with melted butter and place them on the broiler pan. Broil the pineapple for 5 minutes on each side so that it is piping hot and golden.

To serve, arrange the chicken on a serving dish and top with overlapping pineapple slices. Serve with snow peas.

pan-braised chicken

	ingredients	
very easy	2 tbsp olive oil	8 white mushrooms, sliced thinly
	2 chicken leg quarters	1 garlic clove, crushed
serves 2	1 small onion, chopped roughly	1 small fresh chile, seeded and diced
	4 tomatoes, diced	or ½ tsp chili flakes (optional)
	3 tbsp diced red bell pepper	1 tsp dried oregano or basil
10 minutes	1 small zucchini, sliced thinly	salt and pepper
	or diced	scant 1 cup chicken stock
60 minutes		

Heat the oil over high heat in a large skillet. Sauté the chicken for about 5 minutes, skin side down, until golden brown. Turn and brown the second side.

Add the onion, tomatoes, bell pepper, zucchini, mushrooms, garlic, and chile or chili flakes, if using. Sprinkle in the herbs and season to taste with salt and pepper. Mix well.

Pour in the stock, bring to a boil, then reduce the heat so that the liquid is just simmering. Cover the skillet and cook for 45 minutes, turning the chicken occasionally.

Transfer the chicken to a serving dish and keep it warm in a low oven. Increase the heat to high and boil the sauce hard so that it thickens and reduces. Spoon it over the chicken and serve.

crispy crumb turkey

		ingredients	
very easy	1 large boned turkey breast fillet	2 heaping tbsp fresh white
	1 heaping tbsp all-purpose flour	bread crumbs
serves 1	salt and pepper	2 tbsp vegetable oil
	1 egg, beaten	
10 minutes		
10 minutes		

Place the turkey fillet between 2 sheets of waxed paper and beat with a mallet or rolling pin to flatten.

Season the flour with salt and pepper. Remove the paper from the turkey and dredge the fillet in flour. Gently shake off any excess.

Dip the turkey in the egg and then in the crumbs, taking care that it is well coated.

Heat the oil over high heat in a shallow skillet. Fry the turkey for about 5 minutes, or until golden, then turn and continue frying until the second side is golden. Remove from the skillet and drain on paper towels before serving.

✳ spicy bell pepper chicken

	ingredients	
very easy	2 boneless chicken breast portions *Mc/u*	SAUCE
	3 tbsp cornstarch	½ cup dark soy sauce
serves 2	2 tbsp oil	½ cup water
	1 green bell pepper, diced	3 tbsp white wine vinegar
	3 garlic cloves, finely chopped	2 tsp sugar
10 minutes	5 or 6 scallions, chopped	
	¼ tsp cayenne pepper	
15 minutes		

Cut the chicken into bite-size pieces. Place them in a mixing bowl, sprinkle with cornstarch, and toss to coat.

To make the sauce, combine the soy sauce, water, vinegar, and sugar in a small bowl.

Heat the oil over high heat in a wok or pan large enough to hold the sauce and chicken. Stir-fry the chicken, bell pepper, and garlic for about 5 minutes, or until the meat is lightly browned.

Add the sauce mixture, reduce the heat, cover, and cook gently for about 5 minutes.

Stir in the scallions and cayenne pepper. Remove the lid from the pan and continue to cook over moderate heat for 3 more minutes to combine the flavors.

seared duck breast
with orange honey glaze

		ingredients
very easy		1 boneless duck breast
serves 1		SAUCE 1 tbsp honey ½ tbsp orange juice ½ tsp soy sauce
5 minutes		
30 minutes		

Score the skin of the duck breast diagonally at 1 inch/2.5 cm intervals. Preheat the oven to 400°F/200°C.

Heat a heavy griddle until it is smoking. Place the duck on the griddle, skin side down, and cook over high heat for 5 minutes, or until starting to brown. Turn, reduce the heat, and cook over medium heat for 5 minutes more.

Transfer the duck to a roasting pan, skin side up, and put the pan into the oven for 15 minutes.

While the duck is cooking, combine the honey, orange juice, and soy sauce to make the sauce for glazing.

Remove the duck from the oven, pour the sauce over it, and return to the oven for a further 5 minutes.

Serve the duck breast whole or thinly sliced, cut at an angle.

belgian endive, orange & turkey salad

		ingredients	
extremely easy		2 heads Belgian endive	DRESSING
		2 oranges	6 tbsp oil
serves 2		scant ½ cup strips of cooked turkey	3 tbsp orange juice
			pinch of sugar
			pinch of mustard powder
10 minutes + 1 hour to chill			salt and pepper
—			

Remove the outer leaves from the Belgian endive and slice them thinly widthwise. Peel the oranges and slice thinly against the grain, removing all the seeds.

Combine the Belgian endive and orange in a large mixing bowl.

To make the dressing, combine the oil, orange juice, sugar, mustard, salt, and pepper in a jar with a tight-fitting lid, then screw on the lid, and shake well. Pour the dressing over the Belgian endive and orange, toss well to blend, cover with plastic wrap, and chill for at least 1 hour.

Remove the salad from the refrigerator 10 minutes before serving. Toss once more, if desired, then arrange on attractive plates, and sprinkle the turkey strips on top.

broiled mexican chicken

		ingredients	
very easy	2 skinless, boneless chicken breast portions	SERVING SUGGESTIONS
serves 2	juice of 1 lemon	sour cream
	2 tbsp olive oil	guacamole
	1 small onion, sliced thinly	refried beans
10 minutes + 30 minutes to chill	1 small red bell pepper, seeded and sliced thinly	grated cheese shredded lettuce
	1 small green bell pepper, seeded and sliced thinly	jalapeño chiles salsa
15 minutes	1 tsp chili powder	tortillas, rice, or baked potato
	½ tsp black pepper	

Cut each chicken portion into 4 strips lengthwise. Place in a dish, sprinkle with lemon juice, mix, cover, and chill for 30 minutes.

Heat 1 tablespoonful of olive oil on high on a heavy griddle and toss on the onion and bell peppers. Cook over medium heat for 3 minutes, then sprinkle with chili powder, and mix well. Cook for 2 minutes more, then transfer to a warm serving dish.

Remove the chicken from the refrigerator and discard the lemon juice. Sprinkle with black pepper. Heat the remaining olive oil over high heat on the griddle and toss on the chicken. Cook, stirring frequently, for about 5 minutes.

Return the vegetables to the pan and cook for 3–4 minutes to combine the flavors.

Serve the chicken and vegetables immediately, accompanied by any or all of the serving suggestions listed above.

meat

Many cuts of meat are ideal for those occasions when you are cooking for one and short of time. Most steaks, cutlets, and chops can be broiled or pan cooked, and, like Salisbury Steak or Pork in White Wine & Olive Sauce, will be ready in minutes. On the other hand, when you have more time to wait for your supper, there is little that is more comforting than tender, slow-cooked Veal & Tomato Stew, Lamb Curry, or gently cooked Paprika Pork. And when you have plenty of time for preparation, try the handmade Meatballs & Spaghetti like mama used to make.

chili con carne

very easy	
serves 2	
10 minutes	
60 minutes	

ingredients

1 tbsp oil
1 small onion, chopped coarsely
1 or 2 garlic cloves, chopped coarsely
1 green bell pepper, seeded and diced
2 cups ground beef
1 heaping tsp chili powder
14 oz/400 g canned chopped
   tomatoes
½ tsp salt, optional

14 oz/400 g canned kidney beans,
   drained and rinsed

SERVING SUGGESTIONS
grated cheese
shredded lettuce and tomatoes
guacamole
jalapeño chiles
rice or tortillas

Heat the oil over low heat in a shallow skillet. Stir in the onion, garlic, and green bell pepper and cook gently for 5 minutes.

Add the beef and stir well. Turn up the heat to high and cook for 5 minutes, stirring occasionally. Spoon off any excess fat. Sprinkle in the chili powder and mix well. Continue cooking for 2–3 minutes. Stir in the tomatoes, reduce the heat, cover, and cook gently for at least 30 minutes. You may need to add more tomatoes or a little water or beef stock if it starts to dry out.

Check for seasoning and stir in the salt if needed. Add more chili powder to taste, but be careful not to overdo it.

Add the drained kidney beans to the chili mixture 10–15 minutes before the end of the cooking time so that they heat through with the meat and spices.

Serve with any of the accompaniments listed above.

meatloaf

		ingredients	
very easy	1 thick slice crustless white bread	SERVING SUGGESTIONS
	water, to soak	gravy or tomato or mushroom sauce
serves 2	3 cups ground beef, pork,	mashed potatoes
	or lamb	carrots or green vegetables
	1 small egg	
10 minutes	1 tbsp finely chopped onion	
	1 beef bouillon cube, crumbled	
	1 tsp dried herbs	
45 minutes	salt and pepper	

Preheat the oven to 350°F/180°C.

Put the bread into a small bowl and add enough water to soak. Let stand for 5 minutes, then drain, and squeeze well to get rid of all the water.

Combine the bread and all the other ingredients in a large bowl. Shape into a loaf, then place on a cookie sheet or in an ovenproof dish. Put the meatloaf in the oven and cook for 30–45 minutes, or until the juices run clear when it is pierced with a toothpick.

Serve with your favorite sauce or gravy, mashed potatoes, and cooked carrots or a green vegetable.

salisbury steak

		ingredients	
very easy		1 tbsp vegetable oil	salt and pepper
		1 small onion, sliced thinly	¼ ciabatta
serves 1		4 white mushrooms, sliced thinly	¼ cup red wine or beef stock
		1 cup ground beef	
5 minutes			
15 minutes			

Heat the oil over high heat in a small skillet. Add the onion and mushrooms and cook quickly until soft. Push the vegetables to the side of the skillet.

Season the beef with salt and pepper, then shape into a round patty. Add to the skillet and cook until starting to brown, then carefully flip over, and cook the second side.

Slice the ciabatta through the middle, toast lightly, and arrange on a serving dish.

Remove the meat patty from the skillet and set it on the ciabatta.

Bring the onions and mushrooms back to the center of the skillet, pour in the wine, and heat until boiling. Continue boiling for 1 minute, or until slightly reduced, then remove from the heat, and spoon over the meat patty. Serve immediately.

veal & tomato stew

		ingredients	
easy		2 tbsp all-purpose flour	1 small green bell pepper,
		salt and pepper	chopped coarsely
serves 2		2 tsp mixed dried herbs	14 oz/400 g canned
		12 oz/350 g stewing veal, cubed	chopped tomatoes
		2 tbsp olive oil	¼ cup white wine
10 minutes		1 small red bell pepper,	
		chopped coarsely	rice or fresh pasta, to serve
1 ¼ hours			

Combine the flour, salt, pepper, and herbs in a mixing bowl.
Add the veal cubes and toss to coat. Shake off any excess flour.

Preheat the oven to 325°F/160°C.

Heat the oil over high heat in a large skillet. Quickly cook the veal
pieces, a few at a time, until brown all over. Remove the meat
from the skillet with a slotted spoon, draining well, and transfer
to a casserole.

When all the meat has been browned, add the bell peppers to the
skillet, and stir over high heat for 2 minutes. Remove with a
slotted spoon and add to the casserole. Pour in the tomatoes and
wine, stir once, cover, transfer to the oven, and bake for 1 hour,
or until the meat is very tender.

Remove from the oven and spoon the veal, bell peppers, and
sauce onto a bed rice or fresh pasta.

italian sausages with bell peppers & potatoes

		ingredients	
	very easy	4 Italian sausages, sweet and/or spicy	2 unpeeled medium waxy potatoes,
		1 small red bell pepper, seeded and	cut into 4 pieces
	serves 2	cut into 8 pieces	1 medium onion, sliced thickly
		1 small green bell pepper, seeded and	2 tbsp olive oil
		cut into 8 pieces	
	10 minutes		
	20–30 minutes		

Preheat the oven to 375°F/190°C.

Place the sausages in a large, shallow ovenproof dish.

Sprinkle the bell peppers, potatoes, and onion around the sausages. Sprinkle with olive oil.

Cook the sausages and vegetables in the oven for 20–30 minutes, turning occasionally.

Serve from the dish, while still hot.

pork in white wine & olive sauce

		ingredients	
	very easy	1 tsp olive oil	4 tbsp dry white wine
		1 boneless pork steak	4 tbsp water
	serves 1	¼ tsp dried oregano	6 black olives
		¼ tsp dried thyme	
		salt and pepper	rice or fresh pasta, to serve
	5 minutes	2 tsp lemon juice	
	25 minutes		

Sprinkle oil over the pork steak. Rub in the herbs and salt and pepper to season.

Heat a nonstick skillet and brown the pork quickly over high heat, turning once.

Pour in the lemon juice, wine, and water. Bring to a boil, then reduce the heat, cover, and simmer gently for 15 minutes.

Add the olives to the skillet and continue cooking for 5 minutes more to heat through.

Serve with rice or fresh pasta.

crunchy beef
with hot citrus sauce

very easy	**ingredients**	
	MARINADE	CITRUS SAUCE
	1 tsp dark soy sauce	6 tbsp brown sugar
serves 2	1 tsp fish sauce	1 tsp cornstarch
	1 garlic clove, crushed	4 tbsp dark soy sauce
		4 tbsp rice wine
5 minutes + 15 minutes to marinate	oil, for deep-frying	grated rind and juice of 1 orange
	8 oz/225 g steak, cut into thin strips	
	2 tbsp cornstarch	SERVING SUGGESTIONS
		broccoli or bok choy, stir-fried with garlic
10 minutes		spring rolls

Combine the soy sauce, fish sauce, and garlic in a mixing bowl. Add the strips of meat, stir to coat, cover, and chill 15 minutes.

Heat enough oil in a wok or large skillet to deep-fry the meat. Remove the meat, drain off the marinade, and toss the meat in cornstarch. Shake off any excess. Drop the strips of meat into the hot oil and cook quickly for 1–2 minutes, or until golden brown. Remove with a slotted spoon and drain on paper towels.

To make the sauce, combine the brown sugar and cornstarch in a small pan. Stir in the soy sauce, rice wine, and orange juice. Bring to a boil, then simmer gently for 2 minutes, stirring constantly.

Return the beef and 1 tablespoon of oil to the wok or skillet. Sprinkle in the orange rind. Stir quickly to reheat.

Transfer the beef to a serving dish and pour the sauce over it. Serve immediately with one or two of the other dishes suggested.

paprika pork

very easy	
serves 2	
10 minutes	
1 hour	

ingredients

3 tbsp all-purpose flour
1 tbsp paprika
pinch of salt
12 oz/350 g boneless pork
 steak, cubed
1 small onion, sliced thinly

14 oz/400 g canned
 chopped tomatoes

½ cup sour cream,
 to garnish

fresh egg noodles or potato pancakes,
 to serve

Preheat the oven to 350°F/180°C.

Combine the flour, paprika, and salt in a large mixing bowl. Add the pork and toss to coat.

Remove the meat from the flour, shaking off any excess, and place in a deep casserole. Arrange the onions on top and pour in the tomatoes.

Cover the casserole and cook in the oven for 1 hour, or until the meat is tender.

Remove the casserole from the oven and transfer the meat and sauce to a serving dish. Spoon the sour cream over the top.

Serve with egg noodles or potato pancakes.

beef with bell peppers & tomatoes

		ingredients	
very easy		2 tbsp all-purpose flour	SAUCE
		salt and pepper	½ small red bell pepper, diced
serves 1		1 very thin Delmonico or sirloin steak	2 tomatoes, peeled and diced
		1 tbsp olive oil	¼ cup dry white wine
		1 tbsp sweet butter	2 tbsp lemon juice
5 minutes			
10 minutes			

Season the flour with salt and pepper. Dredge the steak in the flour, shaking off any excess.

Heat the oil over high heat in a large skillet. When it is sizzling, add the butter, and cook until melted. Swirl the skillet around to combine the oil and butter.

Cook the steak in the skillet over high heat for 1–2 minutes depending on the thickness, then turn, and cook the other side for 1–2 minutes. The meat should not be too rare for this dish.

Transfer the cooked steak to a warm serving dish. Scrape the bottom of the skillet with a wooden spoon to incorporate any sediment that has stuck to the bottom.

Add the diced bell pepper and tomatoes to the skillet and mix well. Stir in the wine and lemon juice. Bring to a boil, reduce the heat, and simmer for 2 minutes. Pour over the steak and serve.

cured ham with glazed sautéed pineapple

		ingredients	
very easy	1 thick cured ham steak	TO SERVE
	2 tsp brown sugar	baked potato
serves 1	½ tsp mustard powder	green beans
	2 tbsp butter	
	2 slices of pineapple	
5 minutes		
10 minutes		

Preheat a griddle or the broiler to medium and cook the ham steak for 5 minutes, turning once.

Combine the brown sugar and mustard in a small bowl.

Melt the butter in a small skillet, add the pineapple, and cook for 2 minutes to heat through, turning once. Sprinkle with the sugar and mustard and continue cooking over low heat until the sugar has melted and the pineapple is well glazed. Turn the pineapple once more so that both sides are coated with sauce.

Place the ham steak on a plate and arrange the pineapple, overlapping, on top. Spoon on some of the sweet pan juices.

Serve with a baked potato and green beans.

roast tomato & lamb packets

		ingredients	
	very easy	1 tbsp vegetable oil	1 garlic clove, crushed
		1 large (or 2 small) lamb chop(s)	2 tsp fresh torn oregano
	serves 1	or steak(s)	or chopped rosemary
		4 cherry tomatoes	salt and pepper
	10 minutes		
	45 minutes		

Preheat the oven to 325°F/160°C.

Heat the oil over high heat in a heavy skillet and brown the lamb chop(s) or steak(s) on both sides.

Cut a large square of aluminum foil. Drain the meat and place in the center of the foil. Arrange the tomatoes and garlic on top of the meat. Sprinkle with the torn oregano or chopped rosemary, salt, and pepper. Fold the foil to seal the packet and transfer to a cookie sheet.

Bake in the oven for 45 minutes, or until the meat is tender.

Open the packet carefully so that the steam can escape, then transfer the meat and tomatoes to a serving dish. Spoon on the juices from the meat.

lamb curry

ingredients

2 tbsp oil or ghee
1 onion, chopped
1 garlic clove, chopped
½ inch/1 cm piece fresh ginger root,
   peeled and chopped
1 tsp paprika
½ tsp cayenne pepper
½ tsp ground cumin
½ tsp ground coriander

½ tsp garam masala
1 lb/450 g boneless lamb, cubed
3 small tomatoes
½ tsp salt
¼ cup plain yogurt

TO SERVE
rice or nan
mango chutney or pickle

Heat the oil or ghee in a shallow pan over medium heat. Add the onions and garlic and cook until browned.

Add the ginger and continue cooking, stirring constantly, for 2 minutes more. Add the other spices and mix well. Reduce the heat and cook gently for 3 minutes.

Stir the lamb into the spice mixture and cook over medium heat until the meat is sealed all over.

Peel and chop the tomatoes. Add to the meat with the salt and yogurt. Stir well to blend, bring to a boil, then reduce the heat, and simmer, covered, until the meat is tender. This will take 1–1½ hours depending on the size of the lamb cubes and the depth of the pan.

Turn the curry into a serving dish and offer rice, nan, chutney, or pickle as accompaniments

meatballs & spaghetti

easy	
serves 2	
10 minutes + 20 minutes to make tomato sauce	
30 minutes	

ingredients

1 thick slice crustless white bread
water, for soaking
1 quantity tomato sauce (see spicy
  baked pasta, page 78)
2 cups ground beef
1 egg
1 tsp chopped fresh parsley

1 tsp chopped fresh basil
1 garlic clove, finely chopped
½ tsp salt
6 oz/175 g dried spaghetti

freshly grated Parmesan cheese,
  to serve

Put the bread in a shallow dish and add water just to cover. After 5 minutes, drain, and squeeze the bread to remove all the liquid.

Heat the tomato sauce in a large pan over medium heat. Reduce the heat and simmer gently.

Mix the bread, beef, egg, herbs, garlic, and salt by hand in a large bowl. Roll small pieces of the meat mixture into balls. Drop the meatballs into the tomato sauce, cover the pan, and cook over medium heat for 30 minutes.

Meanwhile, cook the spaghetti in plenty of boiling water for 10 minutes, or until al dente. Drain, rinse, and drain again.

Turn the spaghetti into a large shallow serving bowl. Arrange the meatballs and sauce on top. Sprinkle 2 tablespoons of freshly grated Parmesan cheese over the top and serve more cheese in a bowl on the side.

fish & shellfish

Fish and shellfish are endlessly variable, delicious, and healthy. You can use fish to make anything from a light salad to a hearty soup. You can bake it, broil it, or fry it, and serve it plain or fancy, with a whole variety of sauces. The most important thing is that the basic ingredients must be fresh. Try simple, warming dishes such as Baked Flounder or go for the exotic in Thai Coconut Fish. Produce a sophisticated meal in minutes, such as Goujons with Garlic Mayonnaise or enjoy a cool summer classic, such as Salade Niçoise.

white fish chowder

<table>
<tr><td>very easy</td><td colspan="2">ingredients</td></tr>
<tr><td rowspan="2">serves 2</td><td>4 tbsp butter
1 onion or leek, chopped roughly
½ green bell pepper, diced
1 large mealy potato, peeled
  and cubed</td><td>8 oz/225 g lb white fish fillets
  (cod, haddock or whiting)
generous 1 cup canned corn
2 tbsp chopped fresh parsley</td></tr>
<tr><td>1¼ cups milk
salt and pepper</td><td>crusty bread, to serve</td></tr>
<tr><td>15 minutes</td><td></td><td></td></tr>
<tr><td>30 minutes</td><td></td><td></td></tr>
</table>

Melt the butter over medium heat in a large, deep pan. Stir in the onion and bell pepper and cook until they just start to soften. Add the potato and mix well. Cook for 1 minute more.

Add the milk to the vegetables (except the corn), season well with salt and pepper, then increase the heat until the liquid is just about to boil. Reduce the heat slightly so that the milk is simmering, cover, and cook gently for 10 minutes, or until the potatoes are nearly soft.

Meanwhile, skin the fish and cut into ½ inch/1 cm strips. Add to the chowder and cook for 10 minutes more.

Stir in the corn and parsley. Cook for 5 minutes more, then serve with the crusty bread.

halibut with caramelized onions

		ingredients
very easy		1 tbsp vegetable oil
		½ small onion, sliced thinly
serves 1		½ tsp balsamic vinegar
		1 tbsp butter, melted
		4 oz/115 g halibut fillet or steak
5 minutes		
30 minutes		

Heat the oil over medium heat in a large skillet. Add the onions, stir well, and reduce the heat. Cook for 15–20 minutes on a very low heat, stirring occasionally, until the onions are very soft and golden brown.

Add the vinegar to the onions and cook for 2 minutes more, stirring constantly to prevent them from sticking.

Brush melted butter over the fish.

Preheat the broiler or a griddle that goes on top of the stove. Sear the fish on high, then reduce the heat, and cook for about 10 minutes, turning once. Cooking time depends on the thickness of the fillet, but the fish should be firm and tender when done.

Remove the fish from the heat, place on a serving platter, and top with the caramelized onions.

crispy baked flounder

		ingredients	
very easy			
serves 2	4 oz/115 g flounder fillet		TOPPING
	¼ cup butter, diced		4 tbsp fresh white bread crumbs
	1 tbsp lemon juice		1 tsp dried herbs (parsley, oregano,
10 minutes	salt and pepper		or thyme)
			1 tsp mustard powder, optional
25 minutes			1 tbsp grated Cheddar cheese

Preheat the oven to 350°F/180°C.

Arrange the fish in a single layer in a shallow ovenproof dish.

Dot 2 tablespoons of butter over the fish. Sprinkle with lemon juice and season with salt and pepper.

To make the topping, combine the bread crumbs with the herbs, mustard, and cheese. Spoon the topping over the fish and dot with the remaining butter.

Put the dish in the oven and bake for 20 minutes. If necessary, place the dish under the broiler for an extra 3–4 minutes to brown the topping before serving.

thai coconut fish

		ingredients	
	very easy	4 tbsp vegetable oil	6 sprigs fresh cilantro
		1 shallot, chopped finely	½ cup coconut milk
	serves 2	½ inch/1 cm piece fresh ginger root or galangal, peeled and chopped finely	8 oz/225 g white fish fillets
			1 small leek, sliced thinly
		1 fresh chile, seeded and diced or	
	10 minutes	½ tsp dried chili flakes	
	15 minutes		

Brown the shallot, ginger, and chile or chili flakes in 1 tablespoon of oil in a small skillet for 3–4 minutes. Turn into a blender or food processor. Add 2 sprigs of the cilantro, pour in the coconut milk, and process for 1 minute, or until smooth.

Meanwhile, half fill a large pan with water and bring to a boil.

Arrange the fish in a single layer in a glass dish that will rest on top of the pan without touching the water, then pour in the coconut sauce. Reduce the heat until the water is just simmering, then place the fish dish over the water to steam it. Cook for 10 minutes, or until the fish is firm and flakes easily with a fork.

Just before the fish is cooked, cook the leek in the remaining oil until crisp. Remove from the heat and drain on paper towels.

Transfer the fish to a serving dish, sprinkle with the leeks, and garnish with the remaining sprigs of cilantro.

broiled lemon salmon

		ingredients
extremely easy		4 oz/115 g salmon fillet or steak
		juice of ½ lemon
serves 2		1 tbsp butter, diced
		salt and pepper
5 minutes		fresh parsley or dill, to garnish
15 minutes		

Preheat the broiler to high.

Place the salmon fillet or steak on a rack over the broiler pan. Sprinkle lemon juice over the fish, dot with butter, and season with salt and pepper.

Cook for 10–15 minutes (or until the fish is firm and flakes when checked with a fork), turning once. Cooking time will vary depending on the thickness of the fillet.

Transfer to a serving dish and arrange sprigs of fresh herbs around the fish to garnish.

belgian endive crab salad

		ingredients	
extremely easy		8 oz/225 g white crab meat	DRESSING
		2 tbsp ground sweet onion	¼ cup mayonnaise
		2 tbsp finely chopped red bell pepper	2 tbsp tomato ketchup
serves 2		1 tsp white wine vinegar	pinch of cayenne pepper
		2 handfuls mixed salad greens	1 tsp white wine vinegar
		1 head of Belgian endive	
20 minutes			2 tbsp chopped fresh chives, to garnish
—			

Flake the crab meat and mix in a large bowl with the onion and bell pepper. Sprinkle with vinegar, mix well, cover with plastic wrap, and chill in the refrigerator if not using immediately.

To make the dressing, combine the mayonnaise and ketchup. Season with cayenne pepper. Mix well. If the dressing is too thick, stir in 1 teaspoon vinegar.

Wash the salad greens and arrange in the bottom of a large serving dish or on individual plates. Trim the Belgian endive and slice thinly crosswise. Sprinkle it over the salad greens.

Remove the crab meat from the refrigerator 10 minutes before serving. Stir the crab meat mixture, then spoon it over the greens.

Drizzle the dressing over the crab meat. Sprinkle chives on top to garnish, then serve.

sweet & sour
ginger fish

		ingredients	
	easy	2 large white fish fillets, skinned	SAUCE
		1 egg, beaten	2 tsp cornstarch
		3 heaping tbsp all-purpose flour	1 tsp sugar
	serves 2	oil for deep-frying	2 tsp wine vinegar
		2 tbsp butter	3 tsp sweet sherry
		1 green bell pepper, seeded and diced	1¼ cups water
	10 minutes	5 scallions, thinly sliced	1 tbsp tomato paste
			6 pieces preserved ginger, diced
			1 tbsp ginger syrup
	25 minutes		
			rice and salad, to serve

Cut the fish into large, bite-size pieces. Dip the pieces in the egg, then drain, and dredge in flour. Heat the oil and fry the fish pieces quickly for 3–4 minutes, or until they are golden brown. Drain on a dish lined with paper towels.

Melt the butter in a small skillet and cook the green bell pepper and scallions over medium heat for 5 minutes to soften.

Preheat the oven to 300°F/150°C.

To make the sauce, mix the cornstarch and sugar in a small bowl. Stirring constantly, add the vinegar and sherry, then gradually add the water and tomato paste. Finally, mix in the ginger pieces and syrup.

Arrange the fish in a shallow ovenproof dish. Pour the sauce over it and mix gently. Bake for 15 minutes.

Serve the fish with rice and mixed salad greens.

spaghetti with mussel sauce

		ingredients
	very easy	1 lb/450 g live mussels
		2 tbsp olive oil
	serves 2	8–10 fresh cherry tomatoes
		¼ cup dry white wine
		6 oz/175 g dried spaghetti or linguine
	5 minutes	4 tbsp chopped fresh parsley
	15 minutes	

Remove the "beards" and wash the mussels in cold water to remove any sand, discarding any that are open.

Heat the olive oil over high heat in a large pan or flameproof casserole. Toss in the mussels, shake the pan, cover, and cook for 5 minutes, or until all the shells have opened.

Remove the lid from the pan, shake once more, add the tomatoes, and cook for 5 minutes more. Add the wine, reduce the heat, and continue cooking until the tomatoes are soft and the sauce thickens slightly.

Meanwhile, cook the spaghetti in a large pan of boiling salted water for 10 minutes, or until al dente. Drain in a colander, rinse under cold running water for a few seconds, then drain.

Add the spaghetti and parsley to the mussels mixture and stir well. Spoon into individual soup plates to serve.

baked trout
with fennel

		ingredients	
	very easy	1 medium trout, cleaned but with the head on	1 tbsp lemon juice
		1 large sprig of fresh fennel	salt and pepper
	serves 1	1 tbsp butter, diced	
			salad, to serve
	5 minutes		
	20 minutes		

Preheat the oven to 375°F/190°C.

Place the trout on a large square of aluminum foil and push the fennel inside the fish. Top the fish with diced butter and sprinkle with lemon juice. Season with salt and pepper.

Fold the foil around the fish to make a neat packet. Transfer the packet to a cookie sheet, place in the oven, and bake for 15–20 minutes. Open carefully so the steam escapes. The flesh should be firm and should flake easily with a fork. The eyes should now be white.

Transfer the packet to a cutting board. Unwrap the fish, remove the head and tail, and place the trout on a serving plate. Serve with a salad of your choice.

goujons with garlic mayonnaise

			ingredients
	very easy	6 tbsp mayonnaise	3 heaping tbsp all-purpose flour
		2 garlic cloves, peeled and crushed	oil for deep-frying
	serves 2	2 large white fish fillets, skinned	
		1 egg, beaten	lemon wedges, to garnish
	10 minutes		
	5 minutes		

Combine the mayonnaise and garlic in a small dish. Cover with plastic wrap and chill in the refrigerator while you cook the fish.

Cut the fish into 1 inch/2.5 cm strips. Dip in the egg, then drain, and dredge in flour.

Meanwhile heat the oil. Fry the pieces of fish quickly in the oil until they are golden brown. This should take only 3–4 minutes. Remove the cooked fish from the oil and drain on a dish lined with paper towels.

Remove the garlic mayonnaise from the refrigerator and stir once. Set the drained fish on an attractive dish, garnish with lemon wedges, and serve with the mayonnaise on the side for dipping.

salade niçoise

		ingredients	
	very easy	2 fresh tuna steaks or	8 black olives
		7 oz/200 g canned tuna	6 tbsp olive oil
	serves 2	1 tbsp vegetable oil	3 tbsp red wine vinegar
		14 oz/400 g canned kidney	½ tsp mustard powder or
		or cannellini beans	Dijon mustard
	10 minutes	4 cooked new potatoes, quartered	salt and pepper
	+ 2 hours	⅓ cup lightly cooked green beans, cut	
	to chill	into ½ inch/1 cm pieces	2 hard-cooked eggs, quartered,
		2 tbsp finely chopped sweet onion	to garnish
	5 minutes		

If using fresh tuna, brush on both sides with oil, then sear in a heavy griddle or skillet for 2 minutes on each side. Remove from the pan and cut into bite-size pieces. If using canned tuna, drain well, turn onto a plate, and flake with a fork.

Turn the canned beans into a strainer and rinse in cold water.

Combine the tuna, canned beans, potatoes, green beans, onion, and olives in a large mixing bowl.

Put the olive oil, vinegar, mustard, salt, and pepper in a jar with a tight-fitting lid. Screw on the lid and shake well, then pour the dressing over the tuna mixture and toss to combine. Cover with plastic wrap and chill for at least 2 hours. If you like, remove from the refrigerator about 30 minutes before serving.

To serve, mix the tuna and beans well to blend the flavors and textures. Turn into a serving dish and garnish with the egg pieces.

vegetarian

You don't have to be vegetarian to enjoy the occasional meat-free meal. All-in-one pasta dishes, such as Quick Macaroni Salad (cold) or Spicy Baked Pasta (hot), provide plenty of slow-release energy, while the Spanish Omelet makes an appetizing lunch or light supper. Quick and easy Eggplant & Goat Cheese Baguette or the unusual Pear & Blue Cheese Soufflé will make the most carnivorous among your friends and family think about becoming vegetarian.

quick macaroni salad

		ingredients	
very easy		2 cups dried elbow or other small macaroni	1 tsp chopped fresh marjoram, oregano, or basil
serves 2		1 scallion, sliced thinly	2 tbsp white wine vinegar
		½ small green bell pepper, seeded and diced	6 tbsp olive oil
10 minutes		½ small red bell pepper, seeded and diced	2 tbsp pine nuts
		8–10 black olives, pitted and chopped	1 garlic clove, chopped finely
15 minutes		1 tsp chopped fresh parsley	2 medium fresh tomatoes, peeled, seeded, and diced

Cook the macaroni in a large pan of boiling salted water for 8 minutes, or until it is al dente. Drain, rinse in cold water, and drain again. Turn into a large mixing bowl.

Add the scallion, green and red bell peppers, olives, and herbs. Mix well, then sprinkle with vinegar, and mix again.

Heat the olive oil over high heat in a small skillet. Add the pine nuts and garlic, reduce the heat to medium, and sauté gently for 3–4 minutes, or until they begin to brown, taking care not to let them burn. Stir in the tomatoes and continue cooking for 3 minutes more to warm them through.

Pour the tomatoes and pine nuts over the macaroni. Mix together well. Cool slightly, but do not chill. Serve the macaroni salad at room temperature.

spicy baked pasta

		ingredients	
very easy		TOMATO SAUCE	½ tsp garlic powder (optional)
		14 oz/400 g canned	pinch of fennel seeds (optional)
serves 2		chopped tomatoes	pinch of sugar (optional)
		½ tsp dried oregano	
		½ tsp dried basil	1½ cups dried penne, ziti, or other
		½ tsp salt	large macaroni
10 minutes		1 small fresh chile, seeded	1 cup grated mozzarella cheese
		and chopped finely or	2 tbsp freshly grated Parmesan cheese
		½–1 tsp dried chili flakes	
45 minutes			

To make the sauce, combine the tomatoes, herbs, salt, and fresh chile or chili flakes in a small pan. Add the garlic powder, fennel seeds, and sugar, if using. Bring to a boil, reduce the heat, and simmer gently for 15 minutes. Taste for seasoning and adjust if necessary. The sauce can be made in advance and reheated while the pasta is cooking.

Preheat the oven to 350°F/180°C.

Meanwhile, cook the pasta in a large pan of boiling salted water for 10 minutes, or until it is al dente. Drain, rinse with cold water, and drain again. Turn the pasta into a shallow ovenproof dish.

Remove the sauce from the heat and pour it over the pasta. Add the mozzarella and mix well. Sprinkle with Parmesan and bake in the oven for 30 minutes, or until the mozzarella is melted.

baked ravioli with
tomato & cheese sauce

		ingredients	
	very easy	1 quantity tomato sauce (see spicy baked pasta, page 78)	CHEESE SAUCE
			4 tbsp butter
	serves 2	8 oz/225 g fresh ravioli, tortellini, or other stuffed pasta	2 tbsp all-purpose flour
			½ cup milk
		3 tbsp freshly grated Parmesan cheese	½ cup grated Cheddar cheese
	5 minutes + 20 minutes to make tomato sauce		salt and pepper
	20 minutes		

Prepare or reheat the tomato sauce (see page 78). Spread it in the bottom of a large, shallow ovenproof dish.

Preheat the oven to 350°F/180°C.

Meanwhile, cook the pasta in a large pan of boiling salted water for 3 minutes. Drain, rinse with cold water, and drain again. Turn into the dish containing the tomato sauce.

Make the cheese sauce by melting the butter in a medium pan over low heat. Stir in the flour until it has all been absorbed. Gradually add the milk, stirring constantly, and cook over medium heat, still stirring, to thicken. Add the cheese and continue cooking until it has melted. Season to taste.

Spoon the cheese sauce over the pasta in its ovenproof dish. Sprinkle with Parmesan. Bake for 5–10 minutes, or until the top is golden and the sauce is bubbling. Serve from the dish.

spanish omelet

		ingredients	
	very easy	2 tbsp butter	2 large eggs
	serves 1	1 tbsp chopped onion	1 tbsp milk
		1 tbsp chopped green bell pepper	salt and pepper
	10 minutes	4 white mushrooms, diced	2 tbsp grated Cheddar cheese
	10 minutes	1 small cooked waxy potato, diced	

Melt the butter over medium heat in a large skillet.

Add the onion, bell pepper, and mushrooms. Stir well to coat in butter and cook for about 3–4 minutes, or until soft. Mix in the potato and cook for 2 minutes more to heat through.

Beat the eggs with the milk, salt, and pepper. Pour over the vegetables in the skillet and reduce the heat to low. Cook the egg mixture, occasionally lifting the edges and tilting the skillet to let the liquid run to the outside.

Preheat the broiler to high.

When the eggs are mostly set, with only a small wet patch in the middle, sprinkle the cheese on top. Place the whole skillet under the broiler and cook for 2 minutes, or until the cheese has melted and is golden brown. Serve immediately.

penne with
hot pepper broccoli

		ingredients	
very easy	1½ cups dried penne, ziti or other large macaroni	1 small fresh chile, seeded and cut into thin strips, or 1 tsp dried chili flakes	
serves 2	1 small head fresh broccoli, cut into florets		
	4 tbsp olive oil		
5 minutes	2 garlic cloves, slivered	TO SERVE 1 tbsp chopped fresh basil freshly grated Parmesan cheese	
15 minutes			

Cook the penne in a large pan of boiling salted water for 10 minutes, or until it is al dente. Drain, rinse with cold water, and drain again. Return to the pan.

Meanwhile, cook the broccoli in a large pan of boiling salted water for 6–8 minutes. It should be only just tender. Remove from the heat, drain, rinse with cold water, and drain again.

Heat the oil in a large skillet over high heat until it is sizzling. Add the garlic and fresh chile or chili flakes and cook for 1 minute. Add the broccoli and mix well. Reduce the heat to medium and cook for 2 minutes more to heat through.

Pour the broccoli and garlic mixture over the penne and mix well. Turn into a large serving dish and sprinkle with basil and cheese.

pear & blue cheese soufflé

		ingredients	
easy		scant ½ cup water	⅔ cup milk
		¼ cup sugar	½ cup crumbled blue cheese,
serves 2		1 small pear, peeled and quartered	such as Danish Blue
		1 tbsp butter	1 egg yolk
		1 tbsp all-purpose flour	2 egg whites
10 minutes			
40 minutes			

Heat the water and sugar in a pan, stirring until dissolved. Increase the heat, boil vigorously for 5 minutes, reduce to a simmer, add the pear, and poach gently for 10 minutes. Drain and dice the pear and put the pieces in 2 buttered ramekins.

Melt the butter in a small pan, add the flour, and stir until it is absorbed. Gradually add the milk and cook, still stirring, until thick. Add the blue cheese and stir until melted. Remove the sauce from the heat and stir in the egg yolk.

Preheat the oven to 350°F/180°C.

Whisk the egg whites until they are stiff but not dry. Gently fold 2 tablespoons of egg white into the sauce to loosen the mixture. Fold the remaining egg whites gently into the sauce. Spoon into the ramekins and place them on a cookie sheet.

Put the cookie sheet in the oven and bake for 15 minutes, or until well risen. Serve immediately.

eggplant & goat cheese baguette

extremely easy	**ingredients**
serves 2	1 small eggplant ½ cup crumbled goat cheese
10 minutes	2 tbsp olive oil 2 tbsp chopped fresh parsley
20 minutes	1 tsp coarse sea salt or cilantro
	1 medium baguette or ciabatta

Preheat the oven to 325°F/160°C.

Trim the eggplant and cut lengthwise into thin slices. Arrange in a single layer in a shallow ovenproof dish. Sprinkle with olive oil and sea salt. Bake for 15–20 minutes, or until very tender.

Cut the baguette into 2 pieces, each about 6 inches/15 cm long. Cut each piece in half lengthwise.

Place a layer of eggplant on the bottom piece of bread. Top with goat cheese and herbs. Press the top layer of bread down gently on the sandwich and serve while the eggplant is still warm.

eggs florentine

		ingredients
very easy		1 cup cooked spinach, chopped roughly · 2 extra large eggs · salt and pepper	½ quantity cheese sauce (see baked ravioli with tomato & cheese sauce, page 80) · freshly grated Parmesan cheese, for sprinkling

very easy	
serves 1	1 cup cooked spinach, chopped roughly
	2 extra large eggs
	salt and pepper
5 minutes + 10 minutes to make the cheese sauce	½ quantity cheese sauce (see baked ravioli with tomato & cheese sauce, page 80)
20 minutes	freshly grated Parmesan cheese, for sprinkling

Squeeze the spinach well to get rid of all the liquid.

Butter a shallow ovenproof dish and place the spinach in an even layer over the bottom.

Preheat the oven to 375°F/190°C.

Break the eggs onto the spinach. Season with salt and pepper.

Spoon the cheese sauce over the eggs, taking care not to break the yolks. Make sure the sauce covers the entire egg and spinach base. Sprinkle the top with Parmesan cheese.

Put the dish on a cookie sheet, place in the oven, and bake for 15–20 minutes. Serve immediately.

stuffed eggplant

		ingredients	
very easy			

very easy

serves 2

10–15 minutes

1–1½ hours

ingredients

1 lb/450 g onions, sliced thinly
3 garlic cloves, sliced thinly
⅔ cup olive oil
14 oz/400 g canned
  chopped tomatoes
pinch of sugar

1 tsp salt
4 tbsp chopped fresh parsley
1 large eggplant
juice of 1 lemon
2 tsp dried oregano

Cook the onions and garlic in ¼ cup of olive oil in a large skillet, until soft but not brown. Add the tomatoes, raise the heat until the mixture boils, then reduce the heat, and simmer for 5 minutes. Season with sugar, salt, and parsley.

Preheat the oven to 325°F/160°C.

Cut the eggplant in half lengthwise and place, cut side up, in a large ovenproof dish. Spoon the onion and tomato over it. Sprinkle with lemon juice and oregano, then pour in the remaining olive oil. Add enough water to come to the top of the eggplant and topping. Cover and bake for 1–1½ hours, testing every half hour, pressing down or adding more water if necessary.

Remove the cooked dish from the oven and transfer the eggplant to a serving dish to eat hot. Alternatively, let cool in the covered dish until completely cold.

basic pizza dough
& pizza topping

		ingredients	

	easy	2 cups white bread flour, plus extra
		  for kneading
			6 white mushrooms,
			  sliced thinly

	serves 2	1 tsp active dry yeast 1 tsp salt 2 tbsp olive oil	½ small green bell pepper, sliced thinly 1 quantity tomato sauce (see spicy baked pasta, page 78)
	1¼ hours + 20 minutes to make the tomato sauce	1 –1½ cups warm water TOPPING	2 oz/55 g mozzarella cheese, sliced thickly 2 tbsp freshly grated Parmesan cheese
	10–20 minutes	4 tbsp olive oil 1 large onion, sliced thinly	crisp salad, to serve

Combine the flour, yeast, and salt in a mixing bowl. Drizzle in
1 tablespoon of olive oil. Make a well in the center and pour in
the water. Mix to a firm dough, shape into a ball, turn onto a
floured surface, and knead until it is no longer sticky. Grease the
bowl with the remaining oil. Put the dough in the bowl, turn to
coat with oil, cover with a dish towel, and let rise for 1 hour.

When the dough has doubled in size, punch it down to release
the excess air, then knead until smooth. Divide in half and roll into
2 thin rounds. Place on a pizza pan or cookie sheet.

For the topping, soften the vegetables for 5 minutes in the olive
oil. Spread tomato sauce over the pizza base, but do not go right
to the edge. Top with the vegetables and mozzarella cheese.
Spoon over more tomato sauce, then sprinkle with Parmesan.
Bake for 10 minutes at 425°F/220°C, or until the base is crisp and
the cheese has melted. Serve with a crisp salad.

index